ALLSORTS
IN THE AIR

by Mary Gribbin

Macdonald

Factual Adviser: Dr John Griffiths,
Science Museum, London

Editors: Sue Baker, Barbara Tombs
Teacher Panel: Coryn Bendelow,
Frances Scott, Mary Wilson
Designer: Sally Boothroyd
Production: Rosemary Bishop

Illustrations
Andrew Aloof 8–9, 10–11
Jeremy Gower 12–13, 16–17, 22–23, 26–27, 28–29
Kuo Kang Chen 14–15, 18–19, 20–21, 24–25
Elaine Mills 6–7

A MACDONALD BOOK

© Macdonald & Co (Publishers) Ltd 1987

First published in Great Britain in 1987 by
Macdonald & Co (Publishers) Ltd
London & Sydney
A BPCC plc company

Printed in Great Britain by
Purnell Book Production Ltd
Member of the BPCC Group

Macdonald & Co (Publishers) Ltd
Greater London House
Hampstead Road
London NW1 7QX

British Library Cataloguing in Publication Data
Gribbin, Mary
   In the air. – (Allsorts)
   1. Flight—Juvenile literature
   I. Title   II. Series
   629.132   TL570
   ISBN 0-356-13265-X
   ISBN 0-356-13785-6 Pbk

How to use this book

First look at the contents page opposite, to see if the subject you want is there. For instance if you want to find out about helicopters you will find the information on pages 24 and 25. At the end of the book you will find a word list. This explains some of the more difficult words found in this book. There is also an index. Use it if you want to find out about one particular thing. For instance if you want to find out about dragonflies, the index tells you there is something about them on page 9.

CONTENTS

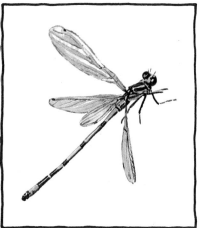

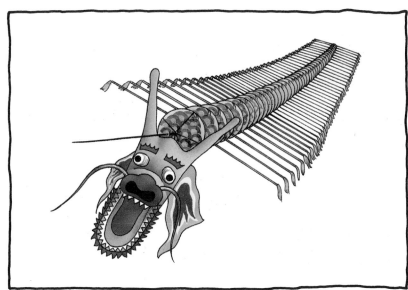

WIND

Can you see the wind? No, but you know when there is a wind because it blows things about. The wind is the air moving. It blows clouds about in the sky, and it pulls at our clothes. It blows smoke from chimneys, and it blows washing on the line.

You can make a light, windy breeze by using a fan or blowing through your mouth. The breeze will be stronger if you squeeze your lips together to make a smaller gap. The wind grows stronger when it has to squeeze through small gaps. When air rushes out of the neck of a balloon, it feels like the wind.

If you can borrow an old umbrella, see if the wind will pull you along on your skates or in a cart. Be careful! It will be hard to see where you are going.

Wind can be helpful, or a nuisance. If the wind is blowing from behind you, it seems easy to ride your bike. If the wind is blowing in your face, you have to pedal much harder.

How does the wind help the washing to dry? Moving air lifts water droplets up into the sky to make the clouds. When the clouds get too full of droplets it rains. Where do you think most of the water comes from?

weathervane

windsock

windmill

anemometer

Look out for these things. A weathervane and a windsock show which way the wind is blowing. A windmill uses the power of the wind to turn millstones for grinding corn or to work a pump. A machine called an anemometer measures the speed of the wind. Its blades turn faster when the wind blows harder.

Fire needs air. When a fire burns, hot air rises up into the sky and cold air is sucked in from the sides to replace it. You can feel the draught of the moving air. But don't stand too close to a fire!

Who has seen the Wind?

Who has seen the wind?
Neither I nor you:
But when the leaves
  hang trembling
The wind is passing
  through.

Who has seen the wind?
Neither you nor I:
But when the trees bow
  down their heads
The wind is passing by.

Christina Rossetti

BIRDS AND INSECTS

Would you like to be able to fly like birds and insects? They often need to fly away from danger on the ground. Birds make nests for their young high up where enemies cannot reach.

Some birds fly a long way from their nests to find food. When the weather turns cold in autumn some birds 'migrate', or fly away to warmer lands. In spring, when the weather warms up and there is plenty of food, they come back.

Most insects can fly too. Many of them feed on plants. By flying, they can reach many blossoms quickly and easily.

Flying is hard work. Big birds like the hawk save their strength by gliding. They just slide through the air without flapping their wings.

A humming-bird flaps its wings very fast. It can hover in one place to feed from a flower, and it can even fly backwards, just like a helicopter.

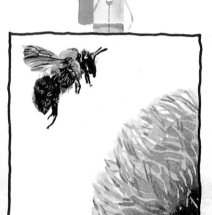

A bee cannot glide at all. If a bee did not keep moving its wings very quickly, it would fall to the ground. A bee flaps its wings so much that they clap together over its back on each beat. This makes a buzzing sound.

Birds' wings have to be very light and smooth. The bones in a bird's wing are hollow. The feathers are hollow too. Feathers make the wing very smooth for the air blowing over it.

Dragonflies are very large flying insects. They have two pairs of wings. Each pair of wings beats at its own speed. You can hear the wings rubbing against each other.

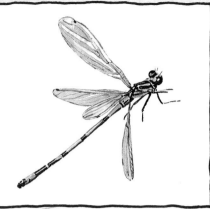

lacewing

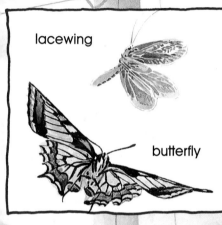

butterfly

Insects have flatter wings than birds. Their wings are very thin and very light. They keep flying by pushing air downwards when they flap their wings. Birds also flap their wings to stay in the air.

moth

fly

ladybird

A bird table is a good place to watch birds flying, landing and taking off. Sometimes birds hover in the air in one place by flapping their wings up and down very fast.

9

FLYING ANIMALS

Birds and insects are not the only creatures that move through the air. But most other flying animals cannot fly upwards, like birds. They can only glide downwards. In a forest they may fly to get from tree to tree without going down on the ground.

Some jumping animals, like the gibbon, swing from branch to branch just as if they were flying. You may have seen them at the zoo. Do flying animals remind you of something you watch at the circus?

Flying frogs have webs of skin between their toes. They cannot really fly, but they can take very long jumps. They can leap the length of a bus.

The flying squirrel has flaps of skin between its front and back legs. When it stretches out its legs, the skin makes a flat wing. Then the squirrel can glide from tree to tree.

Even some fish can fly! They have long fins which they stretch out to make wings. They swim very fast, then shoot out of the water and glide from one wave to the next.

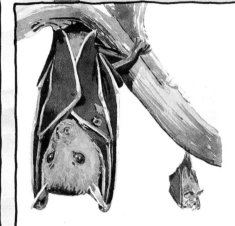

Bats are like flying mice. They can flap their wings and fly like birds. The biggest bat has wings as big as a swan. It is called the Bismark fox bat. The bumblebee bat is the smallest.

Flying lizards stretch their ribs out to turn their whole body into a wing. Then they can glide. Flying snakes also stretch their ribs out to slow themselves down when they fall out of trees.

The first flying animal was the pterosaur, which lived millions of years ago. Some pterosaurs were as small as sparrows. The largest had wings as big as a small aeroplane.

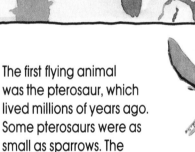

FLOATING IN THE AIR

Watch some seeds being blown about by the wind. How long do they float? Where do they land? Do some of them find good places to grow? Try dropping different things. Does the shape make a difference? Screw a sheet of paper into a ball. Drop it at the same time as another flat sheet. Which one falls down hard? Which one floats gently down like a leaf? The air drags on the flat sheet and slows it down. In a similar way, people use parachutes to slow things down as they fall.

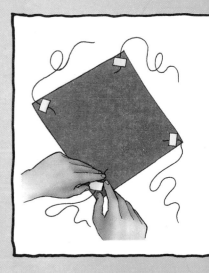

Some parachutists do acrobatics in the air by moving their arms and legs about, before they open their parachutes. This is called free-fall aerobatics.

Have you ever seen free-fall parachutists?

Parachutes are sometimes used to slow down aeroplanes. Three parachutes slowed down this space capsule before it plunged into the sea.

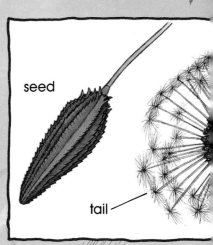

seed

tail

Fix a string to each corner of a thin plastic square. Tie the other ends to a small stone, or a toy car. Throw it in the air. Watch the parachute open and float down. What difference does a hole in the middle of the square make?

A dandelion seed is quite heavy. But it floats in the air because it has a light, spread out 'tail'. The tail is dragged by the wind and holds the seed up like a parachute.

Sometimes a lot of parachutists all jump at once. The record number is 24. They all stand on each other's shoulders and open their parachutes together.

After a parachutist jumps out of an aircraft, he pulls a cord to make the parachute open. The hole in the top of the parachute stops it wobbling as it floats down.

BALLOONS

Do you like watching balloons and bubbles bobbing in the air? Sometimes you can buy balloons filled with helium gas. Have you ever had one and let it go? Did it float up and away? Helium gas is lighter than air. Anything lighter than air will float upwards.

People have always wanted to fly. The first safe way people invented for going up in the air was by hot air balloon. An air balloon filled with hot air will rise up into the sky because hot air is lighter than cold air. People still use hot air balloons to fly today.

Before big aeroplanes were built, huge balloons filled with hydrogen gas were used to carry a lot of people. They were called airships. The people travelled in a cabin hanging underneath the balloon.

When you buy a helium balloon, it is light enough to float away. If you tie an address label to your helium balloon and let it go, someone may find it when it lands and post it back to you.

Eventually, all the helium leaks out. Try leaving your balloon floating in a room. How many days does it take before it touches the floor?

The first hot air balloon flight was over 200 years ago. The Montgolfier brothers filled a huge cloth bag with hot air and it rose up off the ground.

Later they sent up a balloon with a basket hung underneath. It held three passengers – a sheep, a duck and a cockerel.

Some small airships are still used, but now they are filled with helium gas which is safer. They can be used for special jobs like carrying television cameras to film sports events, such as motor racing.

Balloons filled with helium gas are used by scientists to find out what is going on high up in the air. Some of them carry special instruments into the air to help find out about the weather. People called meteorologists study the weather. They use the information from the instruments to make their weather forecasts.

Have you seen a colourful hot air balloon carrying people in a basket hanging underneath? The pilot makes the balloon rise up by sending up a jet of hot burning gas into the balloon. It begins to fall when the gas is turned off and the air cools. A hot air balloon cannot be steered. What makes it move along?

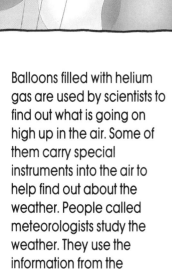

KITES

Have you ever flown a kite? A kite doesn't have wings like a bird or a plane. It is not lighter than air. But it still flies because it is held up by the wind pushing against it. The harder it tugs at the string, the more the wind pushes. You have to hold on to the string tightly to stop the kite blowing away.

A kite won't fly if there is no wind. Sometimes you have to run to make enough breeze for the kite. The breeze pushes the kite up into the air. The highest a single kite has ever flown is 8 500 metres. That is nearly as high as the world's biggest mountain.

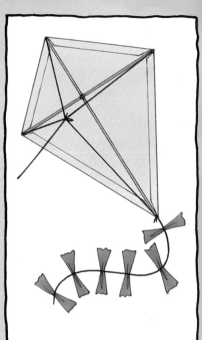

A flat kite behaves like a parachute without a hole in the middle. It wobbles about in the air if it doesn't have a tail to help it balance and hold it steady.

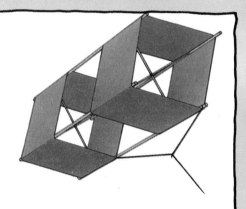

Some kites can balance without tails. A box kite is shaped so that the wind blowing past lifts it like a wing. It flies very steadily.

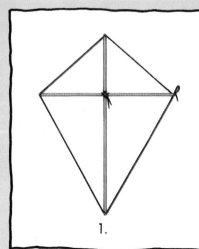

1.

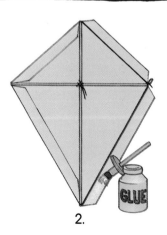

2.

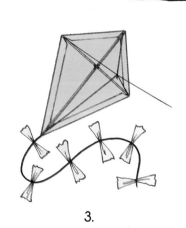

3.

Asian people have used kites for thousands of years to bring them good luck. Some people used to fly decorated kites over the house at night to keep evil spirits away.

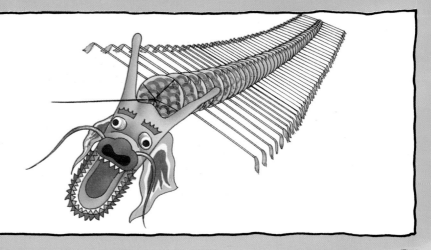

Beautiful kites like this one are made in China. They are painted to look like giant insects and birds. The first kites were invented in China more than 2 000 years ago.

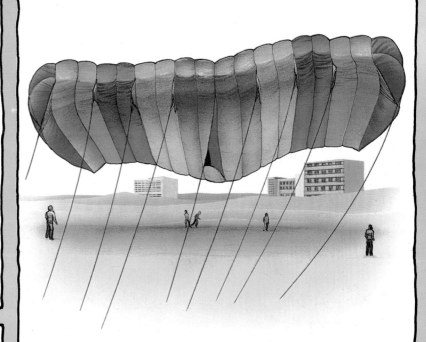

You can make a kite from thin canes or balsa wood tied in a cross. 1. Join the 4 ends with string to make a diamond shape. 2. Glue strong paper to the frame. 3. Make a long tail out of string. You can tie paper bows to the tail to make it fly better.

The largest kite ever launched flew in the Netherlands in 1984. It was very heavy.

It needed 70 people to help launch it and it stayed in the air for over half an hour.

GLIDERS

Gliders can ride on air. They do not have engines so they have to be towed up into the air to get them started. A small plane can tow them. When the glider is high enough, the pilot lets go of the tow line.

Why doesn't a glider fall straight down? If you drop something, it usually falls to the ground. Things fall because of a force called gravity that pulls everything towards the ground. The glider does not fall straight down because it has long wings. The wings moving through the air lift the glider upwards. Wings moving through the air always make a force called lift. The glider comes down to the ground very gently.

Have you ever seen people hang-gliding? Hang gliders usually start from the top of a hill or cliff. Once a glider is moving, it can climb higher in the air. The wings are curved on top. They can make so much lift that the glider goes upwards instead of falling down.

A wing need not be straight. A frisbee is a sort of circular wing! How do you make a frisbee fly?

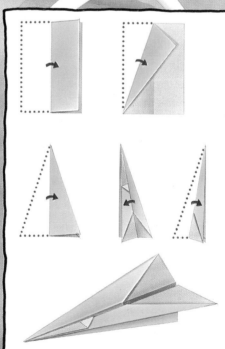

You can make gliders out of paper. Make different shapes. Use sticky tape to make the nose heavier. Watch the paper gliders fly. Which ones fly best?

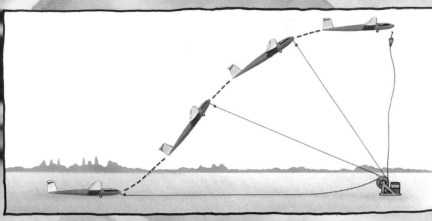

Sometimes a glider is towed by a rope fastened to a winch. The winch winds the rope in very fast. As the wings 'make lift' the glider moves up in the air. When it is going fast enough, the pilot drops the rope.

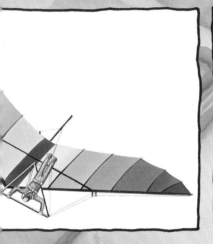

The first human-powered flight was made in a glider fitted with a propeller. The pilot turned the propeller by pedalling, as if he were on a bicycle. The glider was called Gossamer Albatross and in 1979 it flew 36 kilometres across the English Channel.

The first glider that could carry a man was made by Otto Lilienthal in 1891. He launched his glider by running down-hill until the wings were moving through the air fast enough to make it lift.

AEROPLANES

An aeroplane can fly because its wings have a special curved shape which makes the air lift the heavy machine off the ground. It has to be moving quite fast before it begins to lift off.

The first aeroplanes had propellers like windmills to make them move forward. A light petrol engine turned the propellers. Most modern aeroplanes have jet engines to push or 'thrust' them forward. The huge passenger jets use up an enormous amount of fuel when they take off.

The Wright brothers flew an aeroplane with an engine for the first time in December 1903. It was called a bi-plane, which meant it had two pairs of wings.

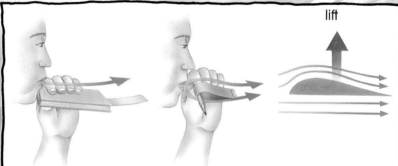

lift

Wind moving past a wing makes it lift. Hold a sheet of paper in a closed book, so that most of the paper sticks out and hangs down. Blow across the paper. Does it lift upwards? The best lift comes from a specially shaped wing, called an aerofoil. It has a rounded top. Air has to move further and faster over the top than the bottom. It sucks the wing upwards.

Try it out. Stick the ends of a strip of paper together and put a pencil through. Blow over it and watch it lift up.

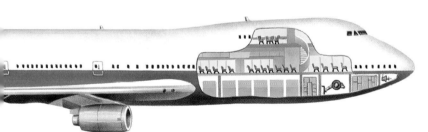

The huge passenger planes used today are called jumbo jets. They can carry over 400 passengers. They are nearly as long as a football pitch and weigh as much as 400 estate cars put together. There are two large holds for cargo as well.

An aeroplane steers by moving flaps, or 'elevators' on the wings and a rudder on the tail. Moving the rudder makes the aeroplane turn right or left. Moving the elevators tilts the plane so it climbs or dives.

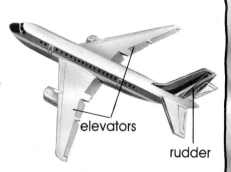

elevators

rudder

When you let a balloon go, it rushes through the air as the air inside escapes quickly through the small opening. A jet engine pushes a rush of air out at the back. This makes the jet aeroplane go forward.

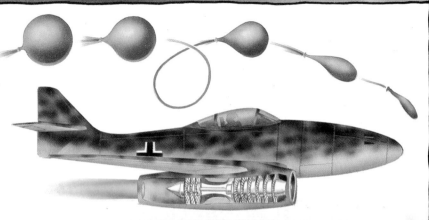

AIRPORTS

Have you ever flown? People wait for their flight in the passenger terminal building. They walk down tunnels to board their aircraft. The luggage is taken to the aeroplanes on trucks. Flying is expensive, so only cargoes that have to move quickly go by air. A zoo once moved a whale to a new home in an aeroplane!

At a big airport aeroplanes are taking off and landing every few minutes. Someone in the control tower signals to each pilot to tell them when to taxi out on to the runway and when to take off. Pilots bringing planes in to land get messages from the control tower too.

Do you know what it is like to be an airline passenger? You can eat, sleep, listen to the radio and get fresh air without leaving your seat.

How many kinds of aeroplane can you spot at the airport? These outline drawings will help you become an aircraft spotter.

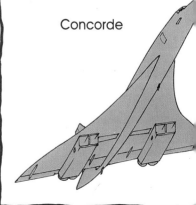

Concorde

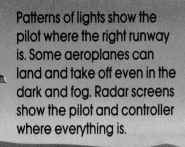

Patterns of lights show the pilot where the right runway is. Some aeroplanes can land and take off even in the dark and fog. Radar screens show the pilot and controller where everything is.

Most aeroplanes are refuelled at the airport. Some can be refuelled in the air through a hose from another aeroplane. In 1958 two pilots flew for nearly 65 days by refuelling in the air.

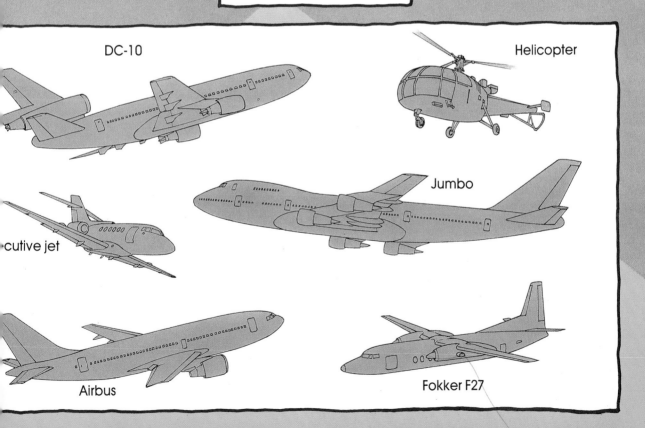

DC-10

Helicopter

cutive jet

Jumbo

Airbus

Fokker F27

HELICOPTERS

Helicopters are useful for special jobs. They can hover in one place, and they can take off and land without a runway. A helicopter can be used to rescue someone from a cliff or a lifeboat, because it can hover steadily. It can lift a heavy or difficult load. Sometimes they are used to lift complete houses.

Helicopters can also be used to take passengers from an airport into the middle of a city. Some buildings have helicopter landing pads on the roof. Helicopters are also used to make regular trips to islands where aeroplanes could not land.

Sycamore seeds are like a helicopter's rotors. As the seed whirls round, its wing 'makes lift' like an aeroplane. The seed may travel a long way before it lands.

The 'wings' of a helicopter are the long, thin rotor blades on top of the machine. They make the 'lift'. The rotor is like a big propeller.

When the rotor spins the helicopter tries to spin the other way underneath. A small propeller on the tail holds the helicopter steady.

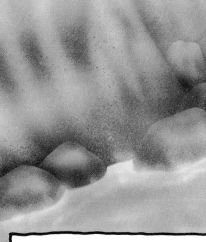

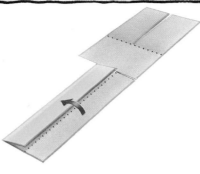

You can make a simple paper helicopter. Cut out a shape like a pair of trousers. Bend one leg forward and one back.

Weight the end with a paperclip. Stand on a chair, throw the helicopter up in the air and watch it fly down, spinning.

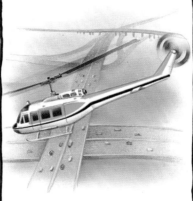

Helicopters are used by traffic police. They can fly slowly above the traffic jams. The crew keep watch on the traffic and report by radio.

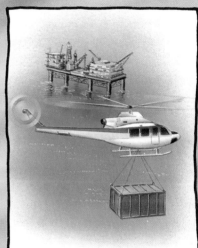

A helicopter can fly people quickly to and from places where there is no room for a runway. They can bring workers out to oil rigs at sea. They can take an injured person from a ship to a hospital.

The Chinook is a very big helicopter with two rotors. One spins one way, the other spins the opposite way. The helicopter is balanced underneath. It does not need a small tail rotor.

SPACE FLIGHT

Spacecraft fly in 'space', above the air. They are pushed up from the Earth by rockets. A rocket works like a jet. A rush of gas shoots out from the engine and pushes the rocket upwards. When the spacecraft is in orbit the rocket is turned off. The spacecraft falls forward, but as the Earth is round it does not fall to the ground. It keeps falling in a circle round the Earth. The astronaut feels weightless – it feels as if there is no gravity! Everything inside the spacecraft must be fastened down or it will float about.

Many satellites circle the Earth. Some take pictures of clouds to help weather forecasters. Some are used to bounce television and radio signals round the world.

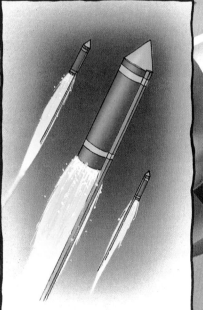

Firework rockets work just like a space rocket. Hot gas is pushed out of the back. The rocket rushes upwards.

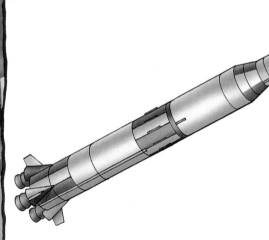

The Saturn rocket was used to take men to the Moon. It was the biggest rocket that had ever left Earth. It was made in pieces called stages. Once the fuel in each stage was used up, it was dropped off. Only a small capsule came back to Earth.

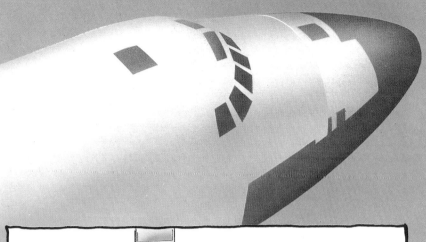

Unmanned spacecraft like Voyager have sent back pictures of other planets, such as Saturn and Jupiter. Perhaps one day astronauts will be able to visit these distant planets.

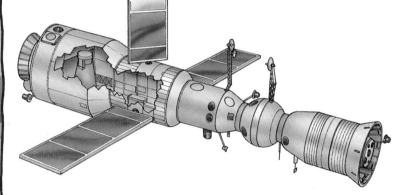

Space stations like Salyut provide a home in space for cosmonauts. They live and work there for months, studying the Earth from space. The cosmonauts carry out scientific tests and experiments. They are floating all the time as if gravity did not exist.

The Moon is much smaller than the Earth. Gravity is not so strong on the Moon. You can jump high, even wearing a heavy spacesuit. But there is no air on the Moon. An aeroplane or helicopter would not work there. The wings could not 'make lift'.

THINGS TO DO

A HELICOPTER

You will need:
2 strips of stiff card
10 centimetres long and
3 centimetres wide,
glue.

1. Glue the strips of card together to make the shape of a cross.

2. Hold the cross by one point and flip it into the air like a frisbee. It will spin like a helicopter rotor as it flies.

3. Hold the cross in the middle and throw it forward without spinning it. Does it fly as well?

A WINDMILL

You will need:
thin card, thin nail,
small bead, stick,
scissors.

1. Cut a square of card.

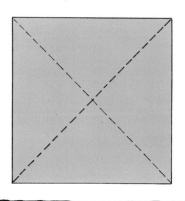

STEERING PAPER GLIDERS

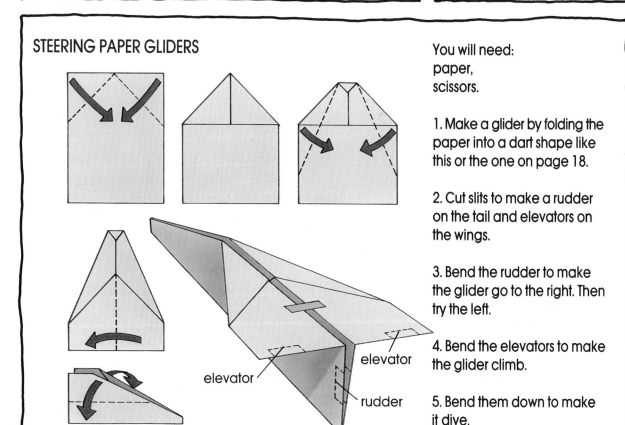

elevator

elevator

rudder

You will need:
paper,
scissors.

1. Make a glider by folding the paper into a dart shape like this or the one on page 18.

2. Cut slits to make a rudder on the tail and elevators on the wings.

3. Bend the rudder to make the glider go to the right. Then try the left.

4. Bend the elevators to make the glider climb.

5. Bend them down to make it dive.

2. Draw two lines from corner to corner.

3. Cut halfway along each line towards the centre.

4. Bend one piece from each corner over to the centre.

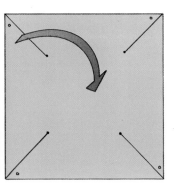

5. Push a nail through all the points at the centre, then through the bead and into the stick.

Use your windmill outside on a windy day or fix it to a bike or run with it to make a breeze.

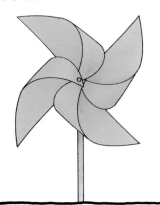

JET-PROPELLED ROCKET

You will need:
1 long balloon
2 small rings,
string,
sticky tape, 2 chairs,
strong clip or
clothes peg.

1. Blow up a long balloon. Close the end with the peg or clip. Tape two rings to it on one side.

2. Thread a string through the rings. Tie the ends to two chairs.

3. Release the clip and watch the rocket fly along the string.

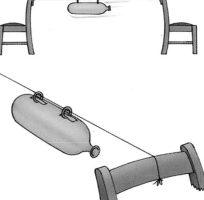

CHAIN OF KITES

You will need:
paper, thin sticks,
glue, scissors, string.

1. Make a kite like the one on page 16.

2. Make another light kite half the size.

3. On a day when your large kite flies well, attach the small kite to it by a long string.

4. When the first kite flies up it should lift the second one off the ground.

5. Let out more string until they are both flying together.

6. Make a chain of three kites if you can.

WORD LIST

aerobatics: doing stunts in the air

aerofoil: the shape of an aeroplane wing

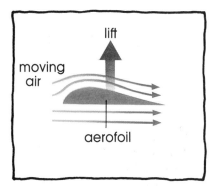

astronaut: a person who flies in space

balsa wood: very light wood used for modelling

breeze: a gentle wind

cargo: luggage and goods carried in the hold of an aeroplane

controller: the person who tells a pilot where to move the plane to, both on the ground and in the air

draught: a rush of wind

elevator: movable flaps on an aeroplane wing used to steer the plane

exhaust: a rush of gas that comes out of an engine

fog: very thick low cloud

free-fall: falling through the air without a parachute

glide: to slide through the air

gravity: force which makes things fall down to the Earth

helium gas: gas that is lighter than air and does not catch fire

hover: to hang in the air

hydrogen gas: gas that is lighter than air and easily catches fire

oxygen: gas needed to make things burn

planet: a body in space that moves round a sun. The Earth is a planet.

plunge: to dive into the water

propeller: a pair of small blades that spin round and drive something along

pterosaur: a prehistoric animal that could fly

radar: a radio system which makes a picture on a television screen showing where ships and aeroplanes are

rocket: something that shoots forward because the fuel inside it is burning and pushing out a stream of exhaust gases

rotor: something that spins round

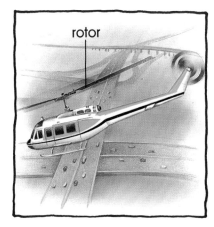

rudder: a fin at the back of a ship or aeroplane used to make it steer right or left

runway: a straight, flat road where aeroplanes can land or take-off

satellite: a small object that moves round a planet. The Moon is a satellite of the Earth.

stage: one part of a spacecraft

tow: to pull along